OPEN

# OPEN FOR BUSINESS

Traditional Shops

Peter Ashley

Everyman Pocket Books
In association with English Heritage

**Open for Business** – Traditional Shops

**Published by Everyman Publishers Plc
in association with English Heritage**

© 2002 Everyman Publishers Plc
Text and photographs © Peter Ashley

ISBN 1 84159 082 7

Design by Anikst Design
Printed in Singapore

Everyman Publishers Plc
Gloucester Mansions
140a Shaftesbury Avenue
London WC2H 8HD

# contents

Shops don't come in neatly ordered sections, with all the butchers followed by
the bakers and then the two candlestick makers. One of the pleasures, particularly
in an unfamiliar town, is that you will find an art gallery next to an ironmonger,
a tobacconist next to a jeweller. And that sense of the unexpected has been
adopted for the progress through this book. Interspersed amongst all the survivors
I have included some shops and businesses that are sadly no longer with us, but
which I fortuitously photographed before their disappearance.

**introduction** *Some shops are still unaffected by any desire for grandeur. They are usually to be found in the side streets; but they are by no means neglected by customers. They are small, low, dark, cosy and warm. Their street-windows may still have the original bow with small panes; but there is no self-conscious antiquarianism about them.*
'County Town', Lynton Lamb, 1950.

The small shops and businesses in Lynton Lamb's eulogy are gradually disappearing from our streets, to be replaced by estate agents, mobile telephone stores and fast food 'restaurants'. This is the age of the retail park, the factory outlet and the customer care manual, where our personalities as shoppers are often swallowed up by somebody's marketing strategy. The identities of small, more traditional shops fight alongside the identikit fascias of the chain store.

This isn't a history of shops and shopping, nor is it an architectural guide to the evolving face of the shop front. It is simply a reminder of the eclectic nature of small businesses – the informal detail, the unpatronising presence – where character and individualism are more important than a remote corporate policy. It is also a record of some of the many things we have lost in the last twenty years.

Cities will always have their Jermyn Streets, country towns their local butchers and bakers, but rural areas are increasingly losing their essential resources. Thousands of post offices face closure, many having already hung up their rubber stamps. It would appear that only those who can adapt to the rapid changes in our society will survive. Those that double up as well used village stores stand a chance, and the Prince of Wales's support of the 'Pub is the Hub' scheme, where you can have a pint whilst buying your stamps and groceries, is particularly welcome. But many have simply disappeared. Some local post offices closed only because they were ordered to computerise, which, in some cases, may have been a bit like telling them to train for a Mars landing.

Just as irrevocably, we are losing the little local garages where we could also fill up with petrol. In 1967 there were 40,000 filling stations. Now it's estimated that it won't be long before that figure drops to 8,000. The problem is that we're not interested in just filling up the tank with fuel and chatting whilst the overalled proprietor checks the oil. No, we also need emergency flowers and giant flaky pastry sausage rolls.

But time doesn't stand still, preserving all the things we love in some sort of bell-jar existence, and if we try to make it, we run the risk of creating an unconvincing simulated heritage. Some of the more popular picturesque country towns are already turning themselves into a pastiche of the very thing they once were, one in particular fast becoming a kind of mail order catalogue shop heaven, where it's easier to spend money on plastic stepping stones that look like hippos than on a decent piece of locally-produced beef. But if we want to enjoy traditional shops with genuine personal service in congenial surroundings, we must use them on a regular basis. We can rely on English Heritage to conserve the bricks and mortar, the decorative tiling, the gilded fascias and mosaics, but whilst we still have survivors in our communities we should perhaps think twice before always driving to superstores. Leave those for bulk-buying toilet rolls and Brillo pads. So go out now and buy yourself a big cauliflower from a greengrocer, or better still, find out where your nearest Farmers' Market is held, where we can once again buy good, local food.

**Smith's, Billesdon, Leicestershire** Even in the late 1970s this was an anachronism. The goods and brands on offer were carefully placed against an extraordinary backdrop of their predecessors. The original Mr. Smith rented the building from the Co-op, and it became patronised by the local ladies of fashion who came here to buy the silk and corsets he brought up from Harrods. His daughter (incidentally one of the first women pilots) kindly allowed me to take the photographs, and the more I looked, the more I noticed just how far back in time some of the items went, particularly the shop fittings and merchandising material. Nothing appeared to have been thrown away, so an empty Carters Tested Seeds dispenser now doubled up as a postcard rack, and the remaining four Tallon ballpoint pens shared space with original tea canisters.

< **Adnam's Wine Shop, Southwold, Suffolk** I first talked about this shop in the *Local Heroes* pocket book, but include it here to draw attention to the quite simply magnificent gilded type for the fascia above the awesome curved window. It's not original – the shop started life as a chemists in 1825.

<< **Bennetts Wine Merchants, Chipping Campden, Gloucestershire** This is how you'd expect a wine merchants to look in this unspoilt North Cotswold town. The main sign strikes just the right note in colour, lettering, and importantly, size, in a scale that respects the texture of the limestone building with its elegant bow window. The neatly chalked blackboard works so much better than the fluorescing stars that usually announce promotions.

### International Stores, Uppingham, Rutland

A transitional moment in the history of the supermarket. The International Stores, once here in High Street West, has all the exterior hallmarks of a shop where you would expect bacon to be sliced for you and sugar to be weighed out into blue paper bags. The fascia is glass and gilt, the moulded corners of the window frames have coloured glass set in them, and the name is spaced out at pavement level in green glazed tiles. Only the trolleys and baskets give it away.

< **Thurlow & Champness, Bury St. Edmunds, Suffolk**

A no-nonsense double-sided timepiece for a jewellers. And have you ever wondered why the Roman numeral for 'four' on a clock is always expressed as 'IIII', when normally we write 'IV'? There are numerous options given, but the one I want to believe is that it dates from Georgian times, when one of the three kings (I'm not sure which) insisted that 'IIII' was correct, and made a right Royal fuss about it.

<< **S.G. Dyson, Oundle, Northamptonshire**

A sun blind pulled out from the premises of a traditional clock repairers. Blinds were a perfect advertising medium, and when I recently took a magnifying glass to a black and white photograph of myself aged two, I was overjoyed to see that the seat of the deckchair I was posing in had been repaired using a canvas shop blind on which can clearly be seen part of the Player's Cigarettes logo.

∧ **Woburn Walk, Bloomsbury, London** A hidden and memorable backwater off the Euston Road, this parade of shops with its identical curved bay windows was built by Thomas Cubitt in 1822 to serve the prestigious Bedford Estate next door.
It was deliberately kept out of sight, the idea being that although you knew that trade went on, you didn't have to watch it happening.

> It's refreshing to see that a graceful parade like this hasn't been turned into a museum piece, but has kept all its Greek Revival elegance whilst adapting to local people's needs. Outside newspaper racks are always fun, particularly London ones like Murray's, with the latest *Die Welt* jostling with *The Scotsman*, the *Socialist Worker* and the *Russian Mirror*.

**South Brink Farm Shop, Wisbech, Cambridgeshire** Out on the fens, produce is often brought straight from the fields and sold in eye-catching wayside stalls. Not often appreciated in architectural literature, they can be superb examples of impromptu vernacular buildings. Near the fenland capital of Wisbech, the South Brink Farm Shop attracts passing trade with a rippling orange pantile roof and bold handwritten notices that shout like friendly market stallholders.

∧ **Store Street Service Station, London**  This little garage has changed colour since I photographed it, but it's still operating at the back of all those furniture stores on the Tottenham Court Road. Sharp 1930s styling is relieved by verdant plants and, happily for me, the seductive curves of a Humber Super Snipe.

> **Norton's, Uppingham, Rutland**  The horse-drawn plough above the door is of the age when this shop saw leather-gaitered farmers walk out with door latches and billhooks. Above Ever Ready window signs are more reminders of services once provided. Set in leaded, stained glass are the evocative words 'Gasfitter' and 'Bellhanger'.

> **F. W. Collins, Covent Garden, London** The same family has run this business in Earlham Street since 1835. A sign tells us they invented Elastic Glue in 1857, and like every serious ironmonger, their products spill out over the street, with ranks of galvanised dustbins, lengths of timber and red-bristled yard brooms. It's the kind of place where you know you'll get a wick for your Aladdin greenhouse heater.

>> **The Whitstable Galleries, Whitstable, Kent** How to have fun signing your art gallery, and at the same time perfectly retain the integrity of the building. The painting on the sail loft doors manages to combine good lettering with an excellent trompe-l'oeil joke.

∧ **South Ormsby PO, Lincolnshire** This is tucked-away England, up on the quiet Lincolnshire Wolds west of Alford. This little building, altered from the original one to two storeys, serves a handful of cottages, farms, and a tree-shaded 18th–century hall.

> **Long Sutton PO, Lincolnshire** Down on the flat, a handful of miles from the Nene outfall and The Wash. 1930s moderne, and although perhaps not appreciated for any overt architectural merit, I think it has great charm, the brilliantly white rendered walls contrasting with the pilasters in light and dark orange brick. Notice the sensitively-placed traffic light control box.

**The Rows, Chester**  As far as shopping goes in England, this is a truly unique experience. Walk along Watergate Street, East Street, and here in Bridge Street, and every few paces you will find steps between the shops leading to a balustraded second walkway, and more shops. They date from the 14th century and are possibly the result of building in front and on top of original Roman buildings.

**Culpin & Son, Uppingham, Rutland** Photographs of shopping streets taken on sunny days were once filled with the sight of sun blinds pulled out over the pavements. For a butcher they were essential in protecting meat displayed in the windows, and Culpin's blind also acts as a red flag as you look down Uppingham's High Street East. When it's closed we can see a window blind and a ruby-red glass name panel.

> **Allen, Mount Street, London**
This is Mount Street Posh, with pink terracotta gushing out from the corner, designed by architects George & Peto in 1886. In the season, one of the best sights in London are the ranks of pheasants and hares hanging outside. Long may they continue to do so.

>> **Elderkin, Spalding, Lincolnshire**
Just off the Market Place in this Fenland town, sportsmen still step in to Elderkin's to stock up with cartridges from under a Brobdingnagian example over the door. Perhaps there's a direct link here to Allen's in Mayfair.

**Much Marcle Garage, Herefordshire** I bet this aircraft-hangar-style garage raised a few eyebrows when it first appeared on the road from Ledbury to Ross-on-Wye. It was built in 1926 as the service depot for the vehicles of Weston's Cider and Perry, a very satisfying mixture of green corrugated iron and wood (the garage, not the cider). A closer look through the windows on the left reveals a pair of original Shell and Power petrol pump globes.

**Walker's, Whitchurch, Shropshire** If you bought
this shop and your name wasn't Walker, I think you'd
feel a pressing need to change it by deed poll in order
to keep the frontage that is still the high spot on the
High Street. Inside it's a fairly routine bakers, albeit
with loaves in baskets and a good line in custard tarts,
but the fascia is worth getting neck-ache for. The name
and street number alone are worthy of attention, with
all that glass and gilt, but look below at the panels at
the tops of the windows. Traditional leaded stained
glass is further enhanced by landscapes painted in
oil on the reverse.

∧ **Eastnor PO, Herefordshire** Another estate village and more thatch. Eastnor has two castles, a roofed drinking well and this post office, but no pub. Temperance campaigner Lady Somerset made sure of that in the 1890s.

> **Docking, Norfolk** A charming hand-painted sign emphasises the importance of the post office as a vital rural amenity.

< **Weekley PO, Northamptonshire** Chocolate-box thatch overhangs the gingerbread ironstone and roses round the door, in an estate village on the edge of parkland surrounding Boughton House. There is something about the sign that is both formal and informal at the same time. Post Office red with a gold Royal cipher, it is a perfect foil to the oversized black tie plate next to it.

**Dwelly's Chemists, Chatteris, Cambridgeshire** Chemists' shops loomed large in my childhood. Even at home there was a permanent display of pestles and mortars and blue containers with gold labels saying things like 'Sul: Praecip'.

I photographed Dwelly's when I popped in one summer afternoon to buy some Dreadnought razor blades, and found much of the interior fittings were as one would have found them eighty years ago. Smart glass display cabinets, bottles on the back shelves and a thoughtful bentwood chair for customers.

> **Montpelier, Cheltenham, Gloucestershire**
> An early sign for a chemists. Now we have a green neon cross, but once it was a large pestle and mortar, representative of the pharmacist's traditional method of grinding to powder the ingredients for a medicine.

∨ **Boots, Ludlow, Shropshire** The only way to do it in Ludlow; because the character of the building has been recognised, there was no need to deface it with a plastic back-lit fascia. The cut-out and gilded wooden Boots logo is perfectly at home on the magpie frontage.

**John Sinclair, Stamford, Lincolnshire** It's details like this that never get mentioned in architectural books, but here I think they're just as worthy of comment as the details on a church at the end of the street. This is a rare surviving example of how shop names elevated themselves with scrolly dignity into more prominent positions, and a reminder that we should always look up above the obvious in the streetscape.

**A. E. Clothier, Kings Parade, Cambridge** This is where you come for all your college kit, whether you're at Cambridge or not (purple and white Kings College rowing caps for punting in Oxford). The window stall board becomes a useful tie rack, and the sunblind is announced as being by Ideal of Putney.

< **Quinto, Charing Cross Road, London**
Charing Cross Road is a mecca for anyone vaguely interested in second-hand books. The walk along the right-hand side of the road from Leicester Square Underground station towards Cambridge Circus is like casting your eye over favourite volumes on a bookshelf. Quinto is one of the best known, both for its corner site with dusty window shelving, and for its appearance in the J. R. Hartley *Fly Fishing* commercial for Yellow Pages. Back home I looked at this photograph and realised I'd missed a Tintin book in the window.

<< **Campden Bookshop, Chipping Campden, Gloucestershire** Another example in this Cotswold town of sympathetic signing and paintwork. Once again there is the utmost respect for the age and patina of the stone building. Even the GPO service access indicator looks at home. Another reward for looking skywards is a 1690 sundial up on the wall under the eaves.

HOSIERS & GLOVERS

**Turnbull & Asser, Jermyn Street, London**
Len Deighton said that he looked in the windows of this crisp shirt shop enough times to feel that he owed them rent. He used to buy Eton College ties here for foreign mates, taking particular pleasure in doing so in his scruffiest clothes. I think that any business still advertising itself amongst other things as 'hosiers & glovers' deserves to be patronised, even if it's only for a pair of socks. Particularly impressive are the fertile cartouches at the corners: flowers, fruits, cherubs and the Cross of St. George.

∧ **Woodward Bros, Stow-on-the-Wold, Gloucestershire** Early morning
condensation slowly dries from the window to reveal slippers and shoes, and
a showcard dispenser for 'Sentry' shoelaces. Sadly Woodwards has gone, but
on my last visit to Stow I was pleased to see that you can at least buy a plastic
dog that looks as if it's burying itself in your garden.

< **Tricker's, Jermyn Street, London** You don't need flashy retail design when
you sell shoes like these. Walking into the shop, it's not the shoes you notice
but the rows of wooden cupboards that, when opened, reveal rows of brogues
and Oxfords in their dim interiors. One of the few Northampton bootmakers left,
Tricker's footwear is synonymous with boardroom wood-panelling and misty
pheasant shoots out in the Shires.

**Beaman's, Audlem, Cheshire** Pear Drops, Midget Gems, Army & Navy Liquorice, paper bags hanging on string, a bell on the counter, and a classic Avery scale for weighing out Uncle Joe's Mint Balls. Not a quaint museum piece in a reconstructed terraced street, but a living reminder of the big-jarred sweet shop tradition. And if all this wasn't enough, out at the back Beaman's make their own ice cream.

**N.J. Stokes, Stockbridge, Hampshire**
A small town in the Test valley, on the A30 east of Salisbury, with two eye-catchers that project their services out into the broad and airy main street. One is the 17th–century Grosvenor Hotel, with its first floor canted bay jutting out on cast-iron supports, and this filling station, with its jolly combination of railway and maritime styles. How pleasing to have attended service from these pumps with their chrome-framed dials and extending hoses.

∧  **Horsted Keynes Station, West Sussex** It was obligatory for every self-respecting provisions merchant to have a delivery bike accompanied by a whistling boy in an apron. Quite how Baker's bike ended up on this Bluebell Line station thirty miles from its home is a mystery, but here it is on Platform One, complete with basket, rod brakes and a leather saddle.

>  **John Graham, Penrith, Cumbria** Traditional grocers often find new leases of life as upmarket food and wine emporiums, but Graham's also recognises the value of retaining and maintaining the original signage. They may not deal in agricultural seed, cake and manure much these days, but the sentiments must still hold good if you're promoting healthy foods.

RAL SEED
E &
ERCHANTS
FAMILY GROCERS
ES AND JOHN
1880
GRAHAM
LIMITED.
FINE FOOD
Fresh Bread
From Melmerby

<< **Great Malvern PO, Worcestershire** 'Post Office Georgian' describes many town post offices, a style very prevalent in 1930s England, and used for many other government offices. It reflected a confidence in the Royal Mail and contributed to an unassailable feeling of civic pride. Here are some examples covering three successive reigns, starting with Great Malvern and George V in 1935.

< **Thetford PO, Norfolk** 1939, and red brick in Breckland, with George VI's crown built into wrought-iron curlicues.

<< **Oakham PO, Rutland** Probably more late 17th century in style, with that scrollwork over the door, but this 1954 addition to Oakham's Market Place is entirely in keeping with the town and the surrounding countryside, particularly with its finely ashlared limestone frontage.

**Hall's Second Hand Bookshop, Tunbridge Wells, Kent** Portable wooden steps to reach high shelves inside, open sash windows to reach shelves facing the street. If you love books, and in particular those that have passed through other hands, this bookshop is one of the best. Established in 1898, Hall's retains much of the atmosphere of that time, happily surviving into this century despite the efforts of a neighbouring bank to try and close it in the 1980s, so that it could have space for an extra cash machine.

**Elsey's, Uppingham, Rutland** Some shops don't need anything to tell you what goes on there. I suppose the meat hanging up in the window is a bit of a giveaway, along with the tiling and the butcher leaning on the half-door watching out for customers. Elsey's, and the green and yellow tiles, disappeared some time ago. Now, instead of shoulders of lamb, it's *Silence of the Lambs*. It's a video shop.

**Eric Ellam, Ashby de la Zouch, Leicestershire** You just know that a request here for one tyre valve would have been just as welcome as one for a Sturmey Archer gear hub. If Mr. Ellam could find one. What is self-evident is that the business of the bicycles themselves is what's important here, no matter how much promotional merchandise was sent to the shop. I can still smell rubber and gear oil; this was a shrine to the John Bull Puncture Repair Outfit and the Fibrax Brake Block.

**Johnson's, Oundle, Northamptonshire** A butcher's shop with a healthy respect for animals, maintaining the sometimes forgotten link between cows and pigs and beef and pork. Illustrative tiled panels were once a common feature on butchers and dairy shops, with Dewhursts using tiles with farmyard scenes by E.E. Strickland until the 1960s. These bucolic scenes date from 1911.

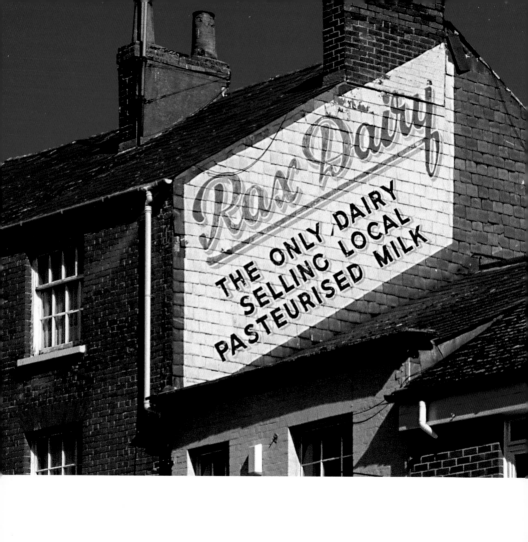

< **Bridport, Dorset** Writing on the wall is probably the longest lasting advertisement there is. This one's kept up to scratch in Bridport on the slate-hung gable, but I bet faint tracings of it will still be visible in 100 years time. There's one on the Old Kent Road in London still advertising a Flickerless Cinema.

v **Somewhere-in-the-Fen, Cambridgeshire** The vitreous enamel advertising sign reached the height of its popularity just before the First World War, and by the start of its decline in 1939, millions had been produced. They were once so ubiquitous that the environment was in danger of being swamped by them, and in the early 1930s their use was regulated. Many examples of 'Street Jewellery' survived until the 1970s when their appeal was suddenly recognised, and screwdrivers and levers were put to work removing them from shop exteriors. It is now very rare to see any in their original habitat, but this perfect Cadbury sign (one of two) was still clinging on in a Cambridgeshire village in the late 1970s. The exact location has escaped me.

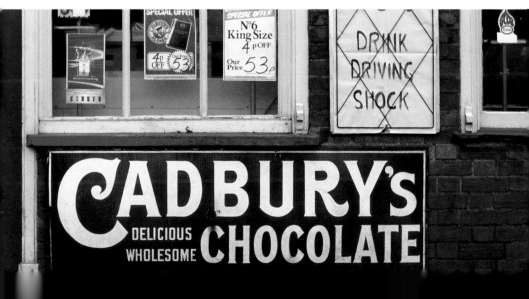

∧ **G. Smith & Sons, Charing Cross Road, London** Amongst the bookshops of Charing Cross Road is this survivor from an age when smoking tobacco was not considered a mortal sin. The glory of this frontage is the gilt and glass used for the stall board at pavement level to advertise cigars, and the proprietor's name on the window. A tobacconists you'd still expect to be selling Kensitas and Churchman's No.1.

> **Bates, Jermyn Street, London** This is where to buy your Equador coffee planter's hat. And while it's being put into a bag you can look at the shop cat that died many years ago but still stares out glassily into the interior. The build up of excess polish on this brass plate on the stall board tells its own story.

> **Martin Wilkinson, Newark, Nottinghamshire** This jewellers was established in 1794, but this exquisite word on the fascia probably dates from around the 1900s. The Art Nouveau fashion for introducing spurious punctuation into lettering has unintentionally turned the capital 'I's into exclamation marks.

# BATES

# SILVERSMITH

∧ **Piccadilly Arcade, London**  Built in 1909–10 by Thrale Jell as a kind of extension to Burlington Arcade, this elegant succession of bow-fronted shops parades gently down from Piccadilly to Jermyn Street, where New & Lingwood's shirts and ties dress up the corners.

> **George Trumper, Jermyn Street, London**  A gentlemen's barbers filled with an atmosphere that can only be achieved by the well-groomed scents of hair oils made with eggs and lemons, anointing unguents and deferential men with correctly-poised scissors. At one time, boys learning the trade in this masculine preserve worked a five-year apprenticeship, practising shaving on an old pig's bladder for the first three.

∨ **Ludlow, Shropshire** These window advertisements usually say something like '–ad–ury's c–co–', some of the thin metal letters having fallen off. Here in Ludlow the message is complete. When I photographed it in 1978 some of the shop goods were also recorded incidentally. The chocolate boxes were getting ready for Christmas and below the round-ended boxes of dates are English Russet apples at 15p a pound.

∧ **F. W. Woolworth, Ludlow, Shropshire** In 1978 Woolworth still had wooden swing doors with elegant curves, brass kick plates and finger pushes, and a glass and gilt sign. Note the Christmas window display and part of a Leo Sayer LP. Inside, the stack of self-service baskets were a clue as to the way things were going, but even at this time the Ludlow branch was very much a lone survivor of the memorable Woolie's style.

> **Kings Cliffe Bakery, Northamptonshire**
Hovis was once one of the most common signs on shop fronts, either in the ubiquitous V-form or, as here, almost a substitute for a fascia board. It immediately says 'baker' and examples are kept by film prop departments to add a touch of authenticity to period English street scenes.

The original name was 'Smith's Patent Germ Flour', which did little for the product, and so a competition to find something snappier was organised in 1890. It was so very nearly 'Yum-Yum', but the £25 prize thankfully went to London student Herbert Grime for his abbreviation of *hominis vis*, which as every Latin scholar knows, translates as 'the strength of man'.

>> **Shoe Repairers, Totnes, Devon** A plain simple shop front that does what it says on the sign. A pink paper notice in the window reminds car drivers of a potential hazard suffered by shopkeepers in the narrow streets of this popular Devon town. Traffic here is often brought to a standstill, and car exhaust fumes drift into shops and attempt to gas everybody as they work, which can't help all the soleing and heeling going on in these unpretentious premises.

**Wadenhoe PO, Northamptonshire**  An Act of Parliament passed in 1869
gave the Postmaster-General the sole right to operate telegraphs, and in 1870
equipment was installed in a thousand post offices. Wadenhoe witnessed the
first telegraph line installed outside of London, for the use of the Rt. Hon. George
Ward-Hunt, First Lord of the Admiralty, at Wadenhoe House.

**E. Smith, Stilton, Cambridgeshire** A late-Victorian option for lettering, off what was once the Great North Road. Stilton was where Cooper Thornhill and Mrs. Pawlett introduced the eponymous cheese from the latter's Leicestershire dairy to coach passengers at Thornhill's Bell Inn. Even more remarkable than the exotic cut-out letters is the survival of the double-fronted bow window, and although the interior is modern, the glazing has still been allowed to turn inside to make a lobby. Just right for stacking a few Stiltons.

**Arnison's, Penrith, Cumbria** A mainstay for ladies of a certain age. The letters flowing erratically across the frontage are evocative of an era of formidable typography, and the descriptive words underneath tell of bales of material measured out on a brass rule nailed to the counter, tailor's dummies and cloche hats. This building was also once home to William and Dorothy Wordsworth's grandparents.

**Mary Milnthorpe & Daughters, Settle, North Yorkshire** This jeweller's shop is remarkable as much for the survival of the original and extremely elegant early 19th–century windows as for the rare alternative to the more ubiquitous '...& Sons'. Settle is obviously well known to those using the railway to and from Carlisle, and its station is another beautiful survivor from a more leisured age.

**John Horsley, Rushden, Northamptonshire** We are all perhaps familiar with the classic Spratt's pictogram, the letters beautifully drawn to resemble the shape of a Scottie dog. Not given the same exposure were other variants seen here – a canary doubling up as a budgerigar, and a fish. There was also a Spratt's cat. They were designed in 1936 by Max Field-Bush. This jolly chirruping, barking and bubbling addition to Rushden's streetscape has now been demolished.

**E. Bainbridge, Farningham, Kent** I suppose it's no coincidence that butchers' shops have cropped up in this book more often than any other. The fact that so many survive is evidence of how we still like to talk about buying meat with someone who knows what they're talking about. Even supermarkets recognise it, and so away from the chiller cabinets keep a jolly butcher on hand to help out. You can't get more traditional than Bainbridge's white tiled shop, sitting at the heart of the community at the end of a row of cottages and opposite a pub.

**The Pantiles, Tunbridge Wells, Kent** This terrace of colonnades and lime trees has something of interest at every turn, not necessarily in individual shops (although there's a fabulous cookshop with cafetières stacked in the window) but in the general ambience. Nowadays, this would be called a shopping precinct, but that's not what comes to mind. An early row of shops here were destroyed by fire in 1687, and the 'walks' were re-paved in square earthenware pantiles, replaced in the 18th century by the existing Purbeck flagstones. There is also a chalybeate well, a shop with a music gallery above it and a Victorian Penfold hexagonal pillar box. But the most encouraging thing is that it is not only still here, but it's lovingly cared for and used by the people of Royal Tunbridge Wells.

**acknowledgements** Above all, I must thank all those kind shopkeepers, traders and their families, both past and present, who very kindly gave me access to their places of business and offered invaluable information. (Or didn't call the police when I struggled to contort myself into physically impossible positions in an attempt to eliminate my reflection from their windows.) Additional thanks to Beaman's and Jean Skinner in Audlem; Gordon Beard at Whitstable Galleries; Bob at Allen's in Mayfair; Ely Tourist Information Centre; Billesdon Post Office; and Lou Wythe for point duty whilst I struggled with a cow and a pig. At Everyman: Sandra Pisano, David Campbell and Clémence Jacquinet. At Anikst Design: James Warner and Misha Anikst. At English Heritage: Val Horsler and Simon Bergin. And elsewhere: James Bowdidge, Margaret Shepherd, Rupert Farnsworth, G.W.R. Ashley and Elizabeth Raven-Hill.

**bibliography** *A Nation of Shopkeepers*, Bill Evans & Andrew Lawson, Plexus, London, 1981. *Shop Fronts,* Alan Powers, Chatto & Windus, 1989. *Designage*, Arnold Schwartzman, Chronicle Books, 1998. *Street Jewellery*, Christopher Baglee and Andrew Morley, New Cavendish Books, 1978. *High Street*, J.M. Richards, (illustrated by Eric Ravilious), Country Life, 1939. *Len Deighton's London Dossier*, Jonathan Cape, 1967.

< **Colmworth, Bedfordshire** About as straightforward as roadside petrol supply can get. I don't think it works now, but long may it remain here.

*Overleaf:*
**Tankerton, Whitstable, Kent** A seaside promenade café, closed for the winter.

Sorry w

CLOSE

An official portrait of the Queen Mother taken for her 90th birthday